BIRDS ACTION COLORING BOOK

Volume #1

By

Nontvaris

BIRDS ACTION COLORING BOOK

Volume #1

Copyright: Published in the United States by Nontvaris
Published july2016

ISBN-13: 978-1535430715
ISBN-10: 1535430710

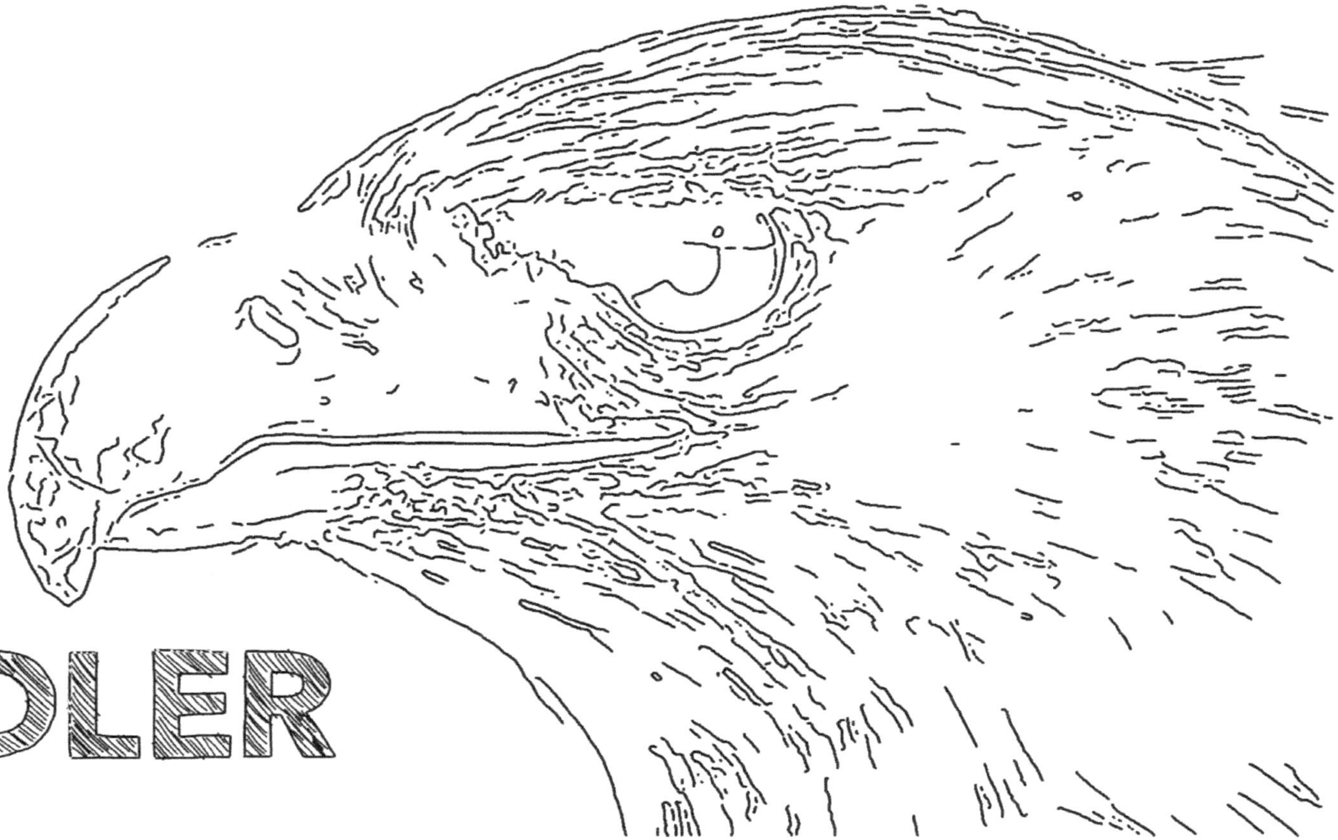

ADLER

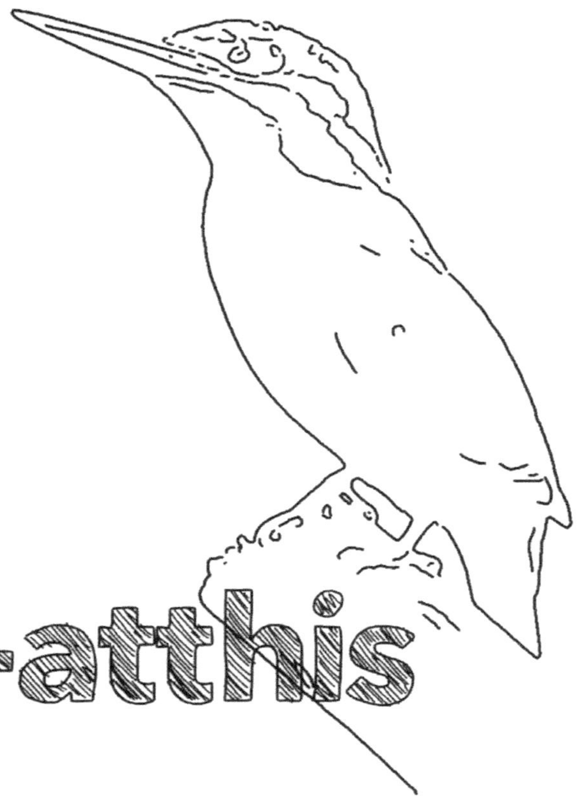

Alcedo-atthis

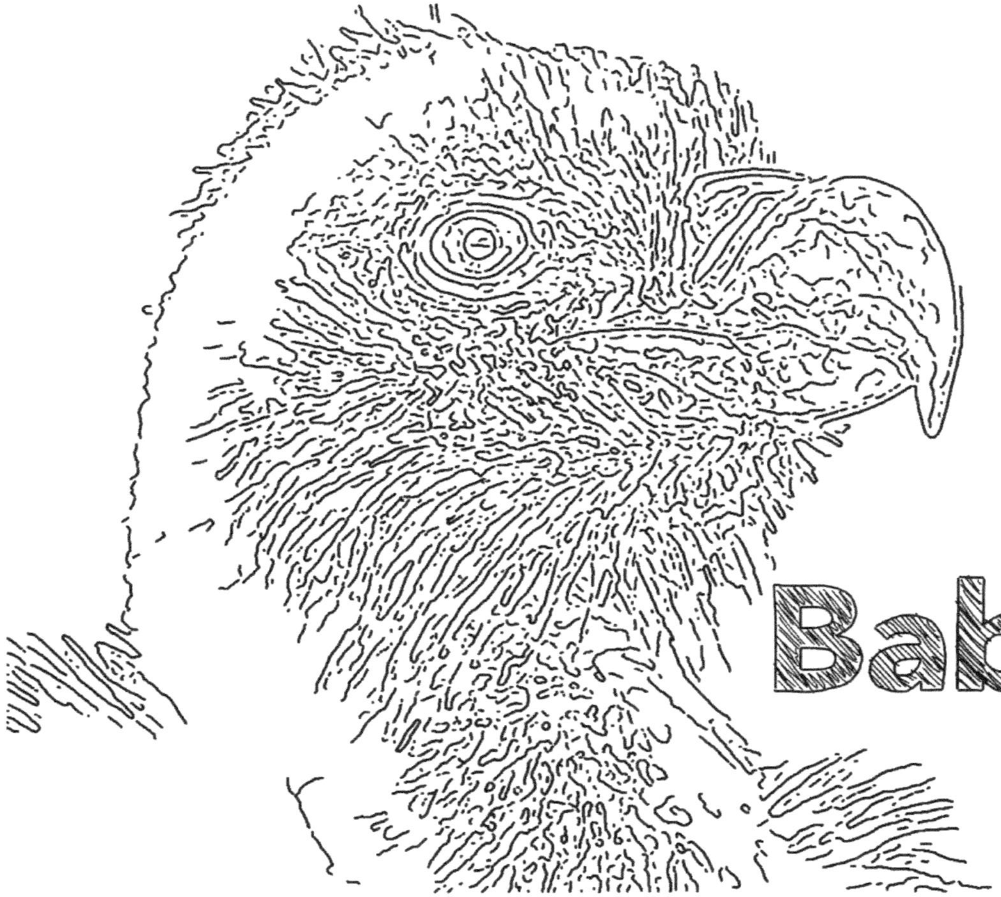

Baby bird

barn-owl

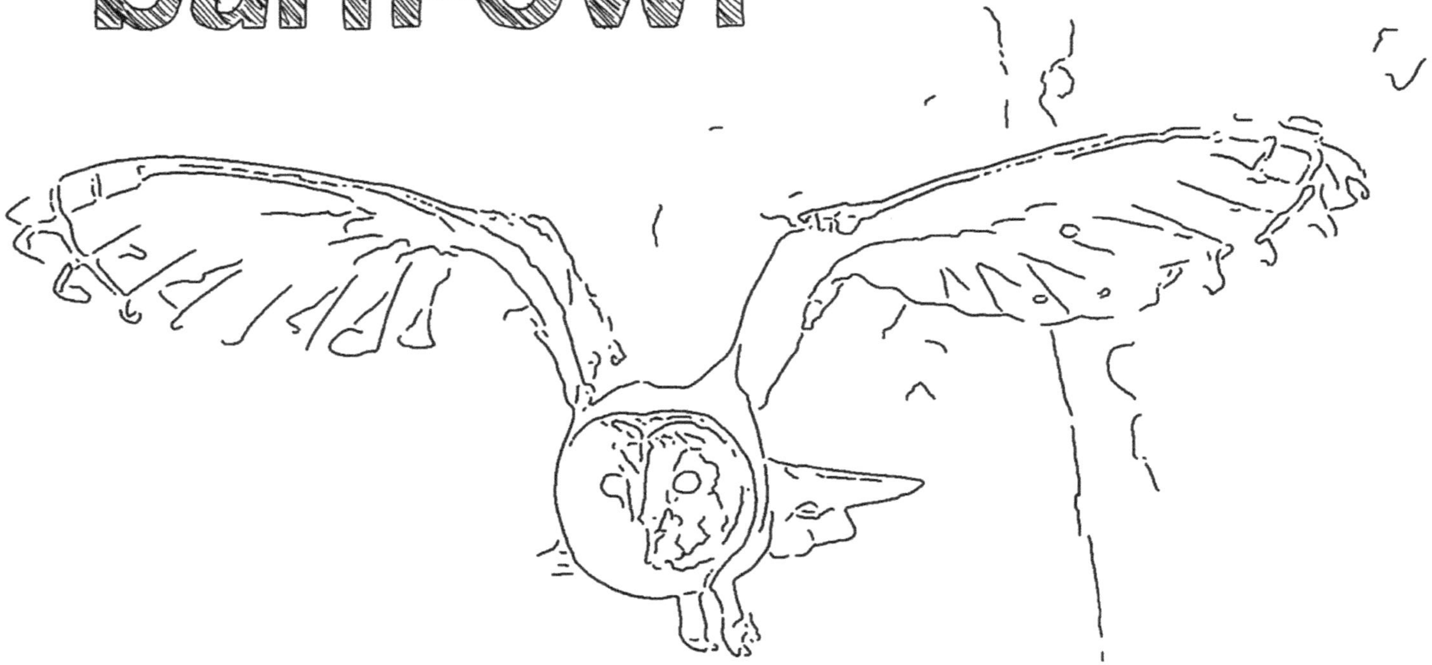

Blue-tit

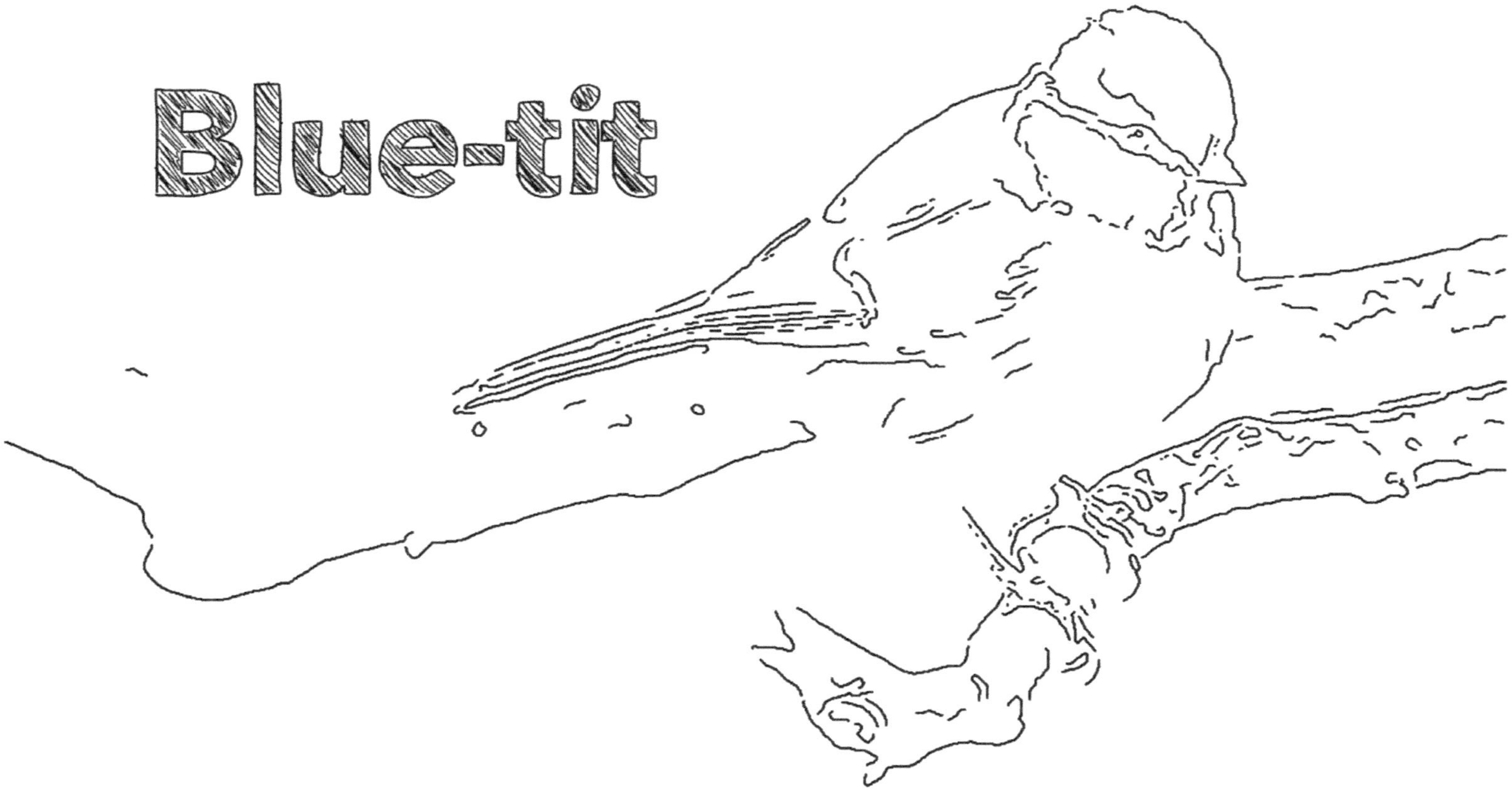

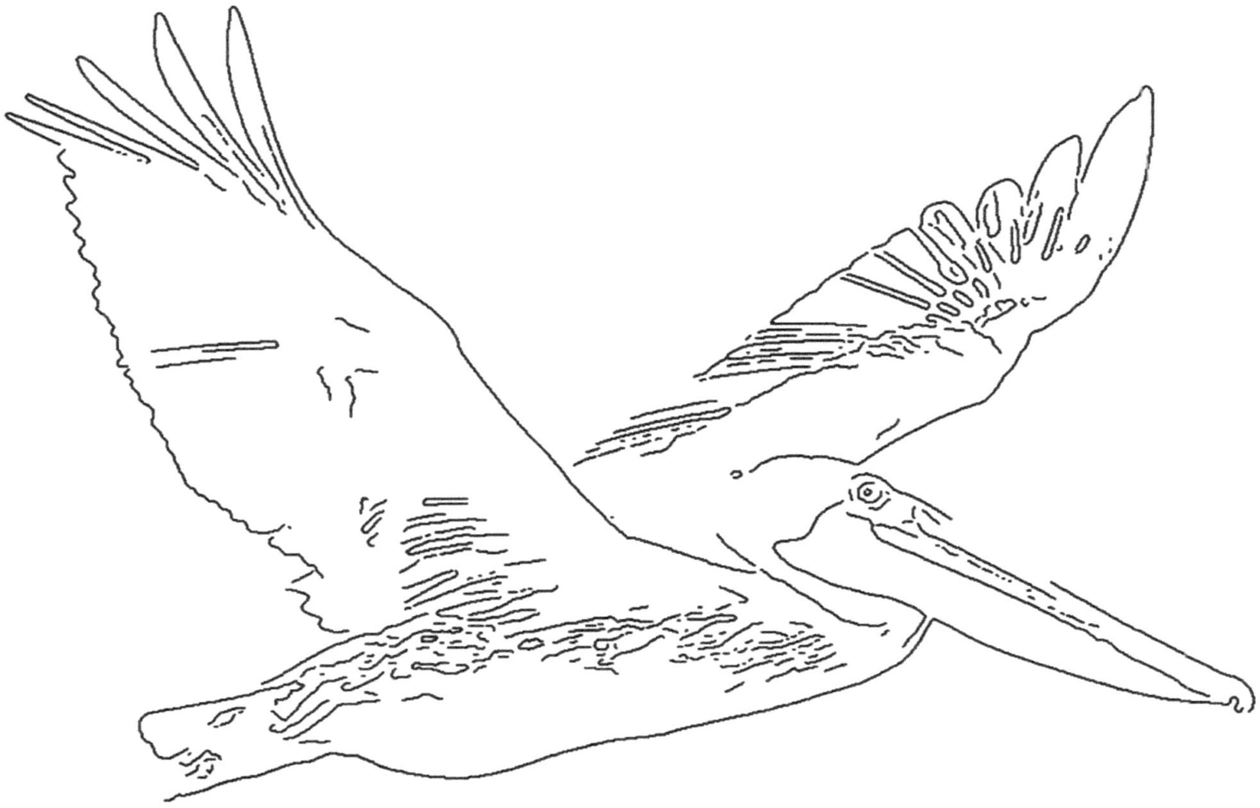

Brown-pelican

Frigate-bird

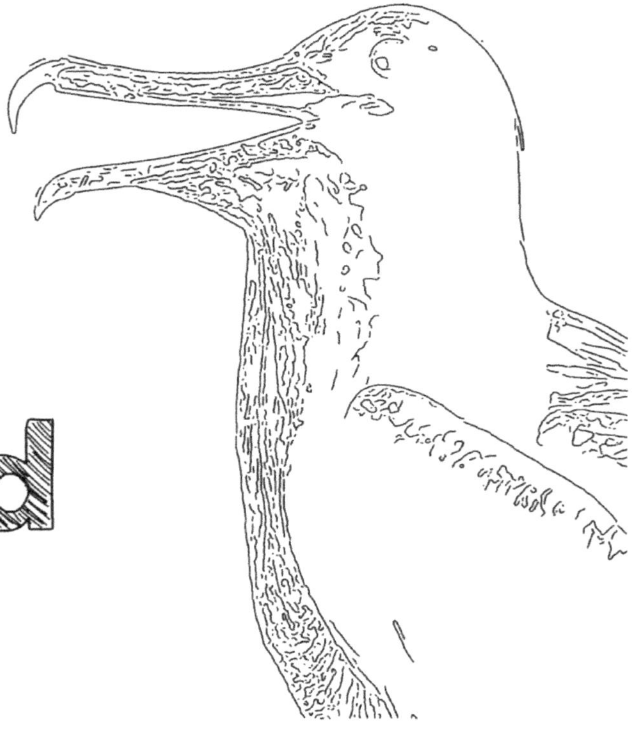

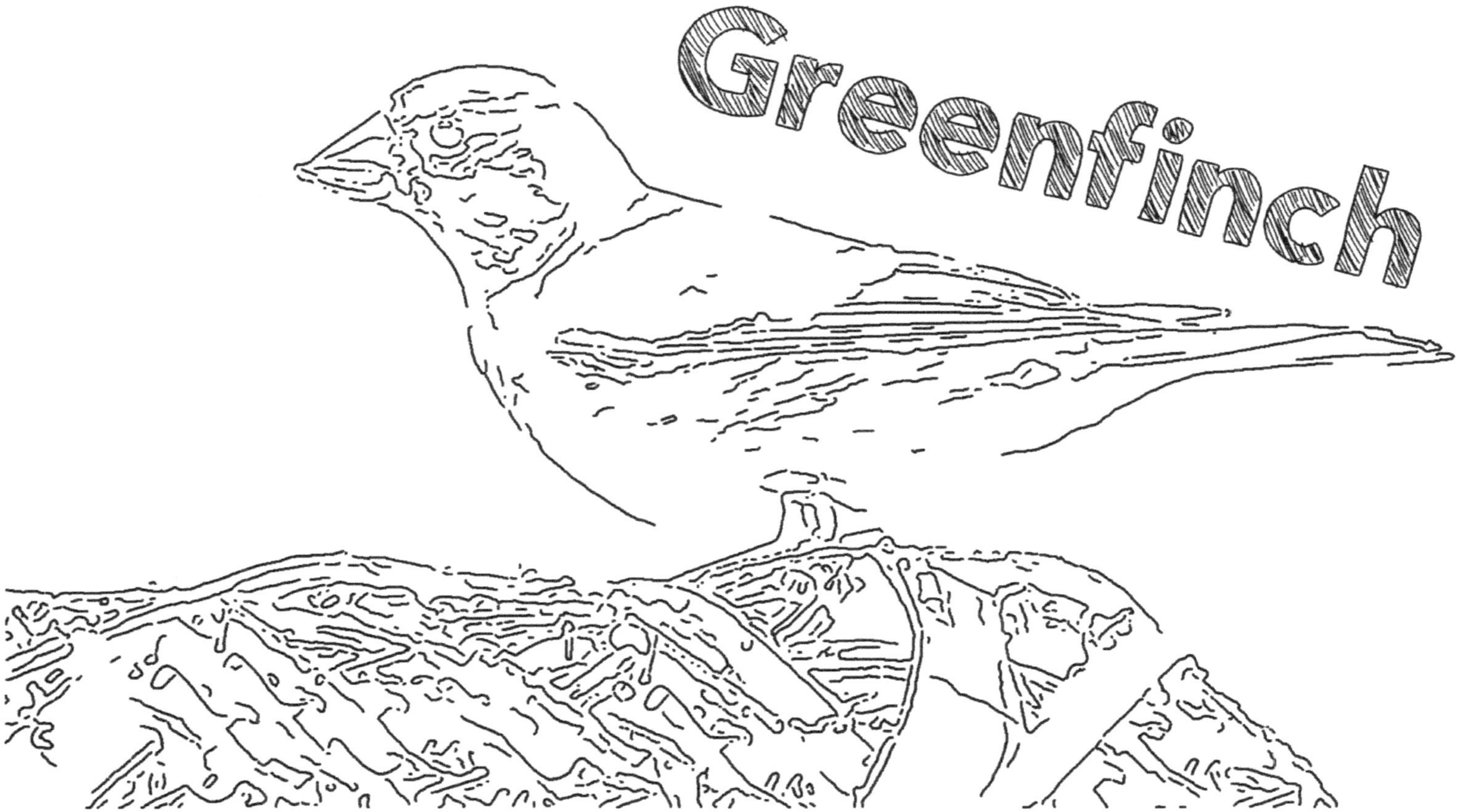
Greenfinch

Grey-crowned-crane

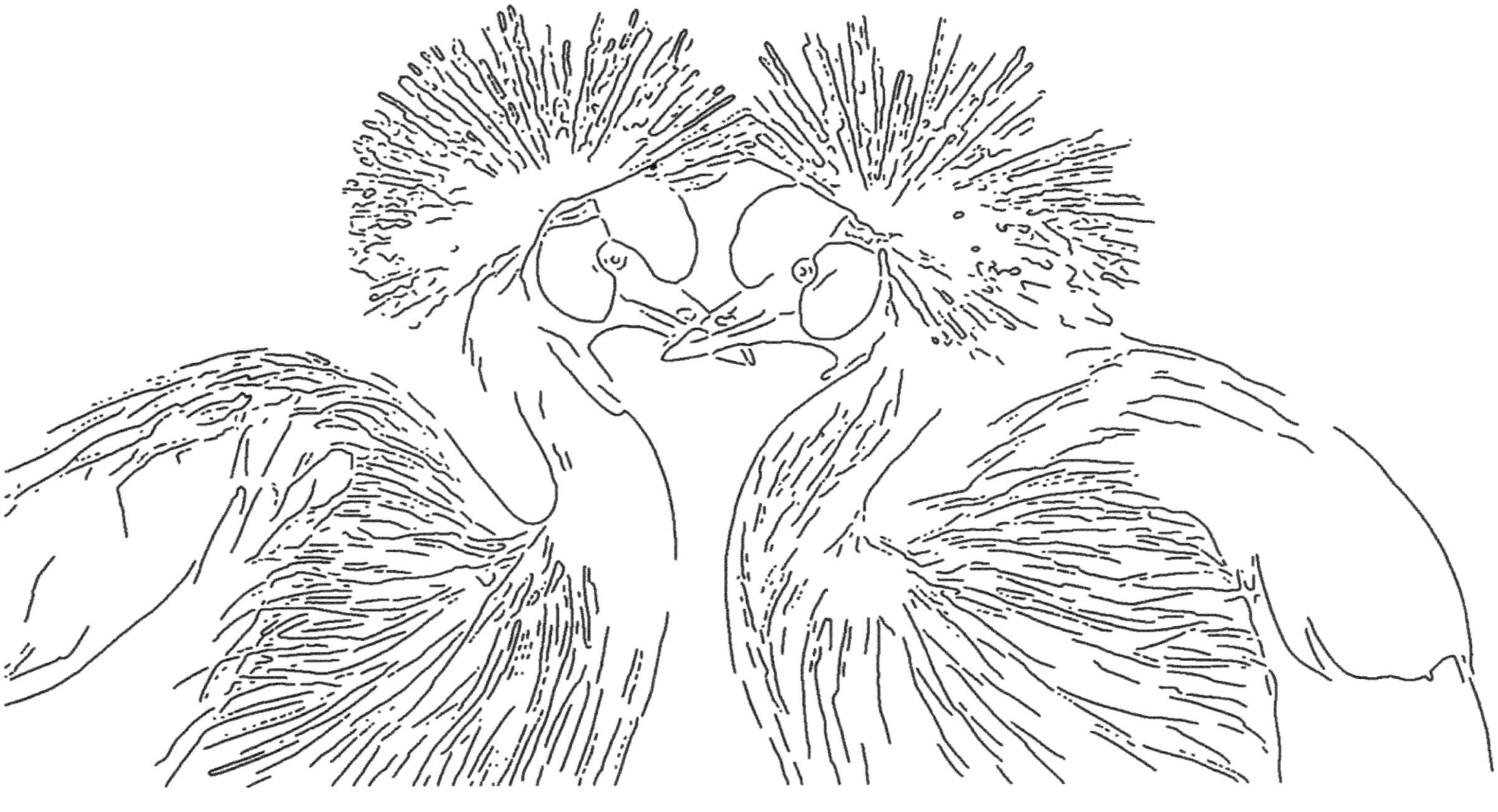

Hornbill

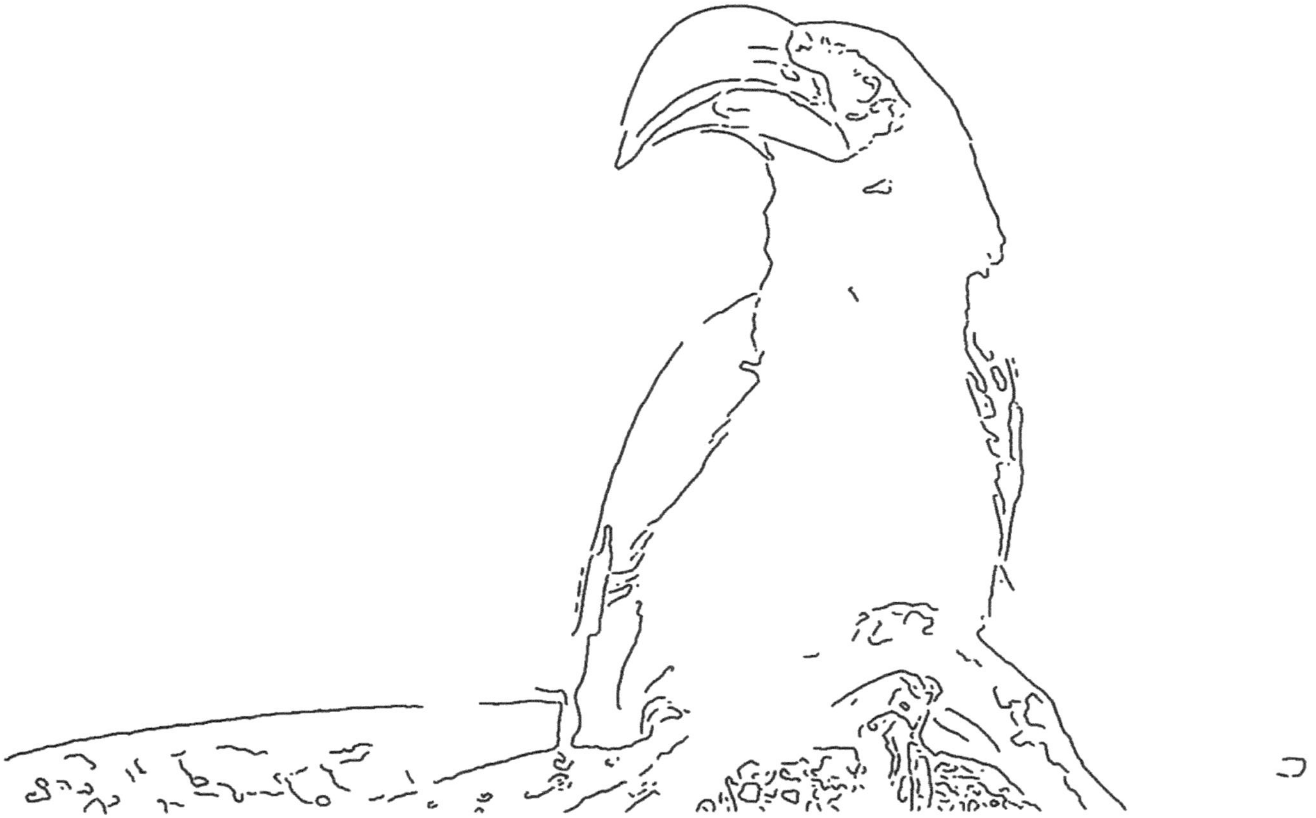

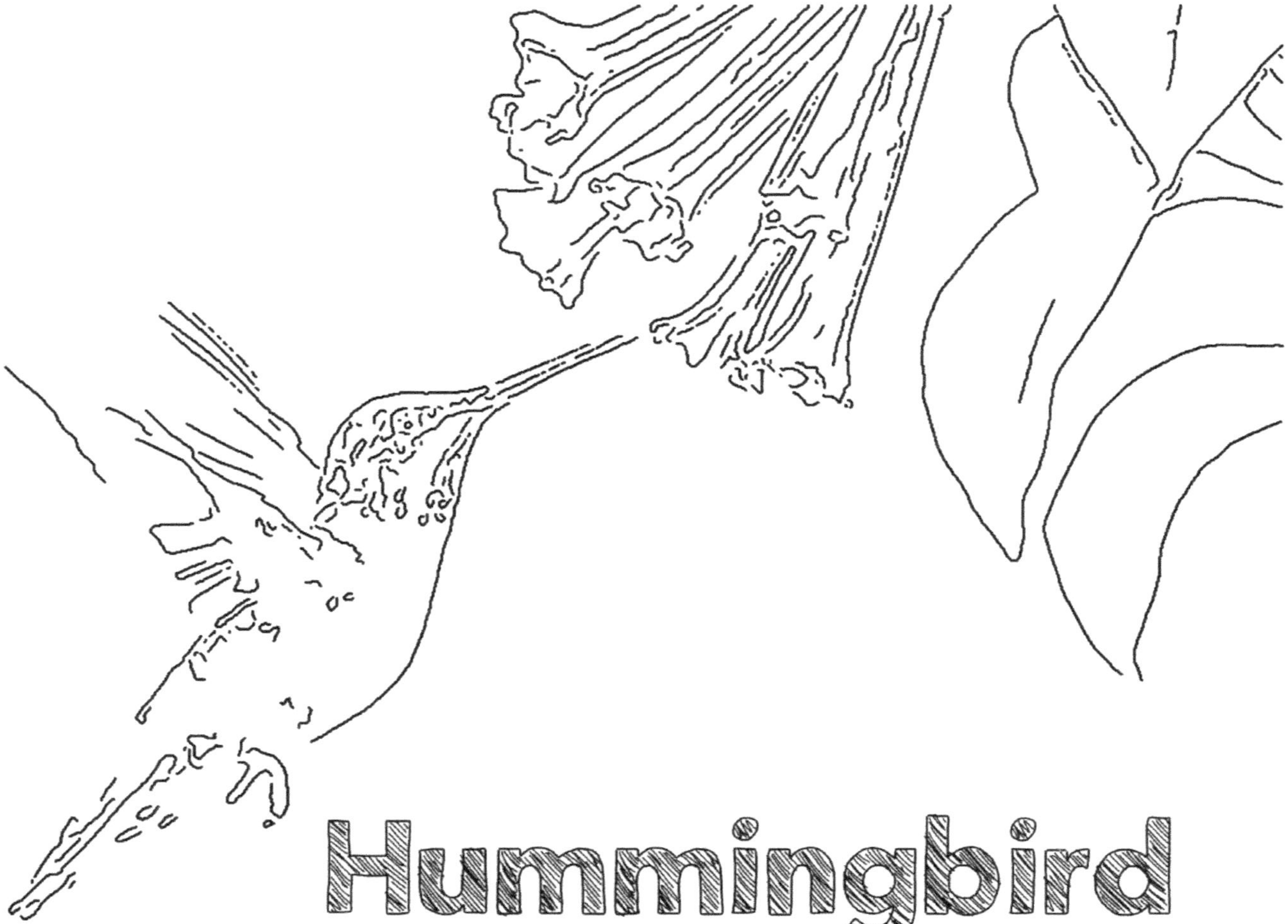

Hummingbird

Merle

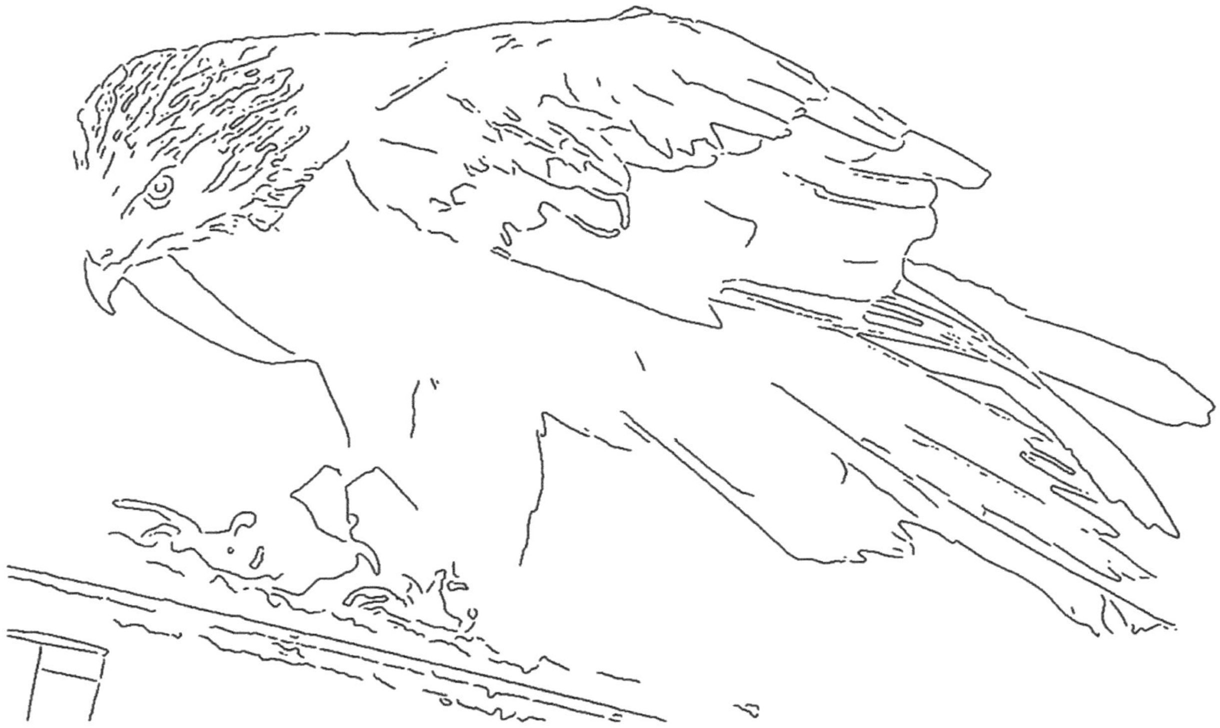

Milan

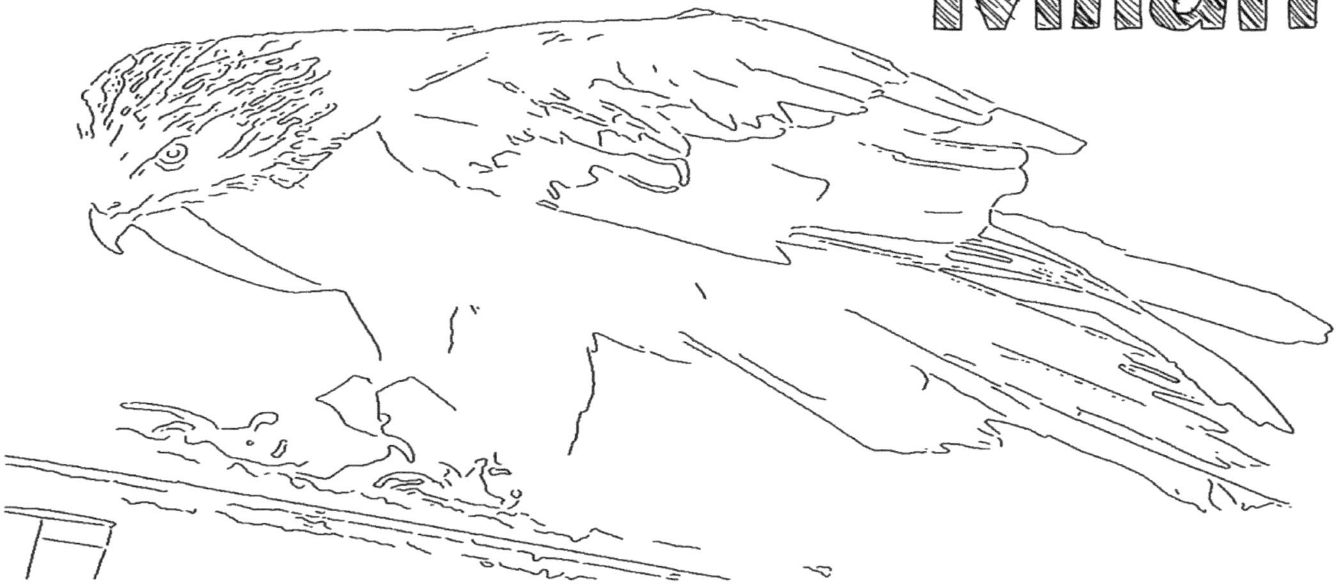

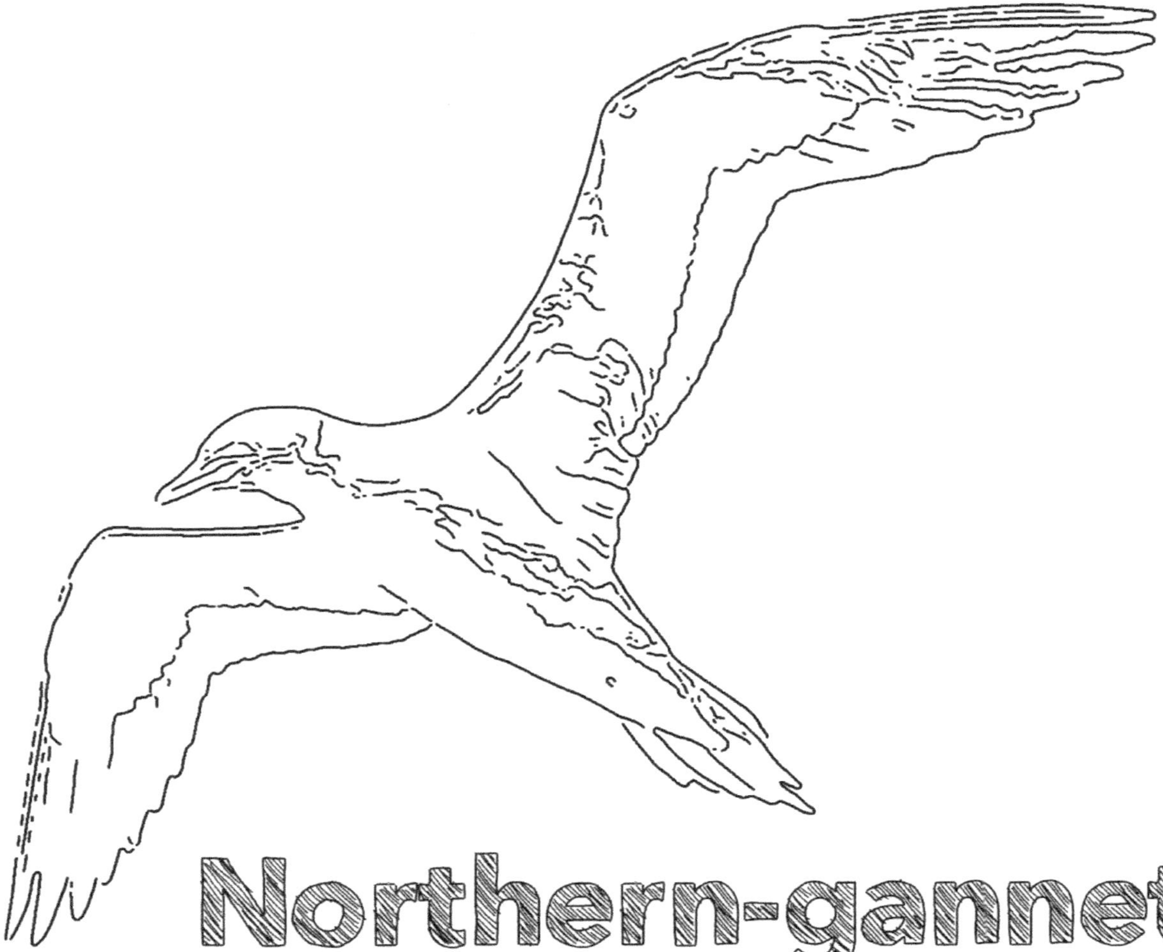

Northern-gannet

Parrot

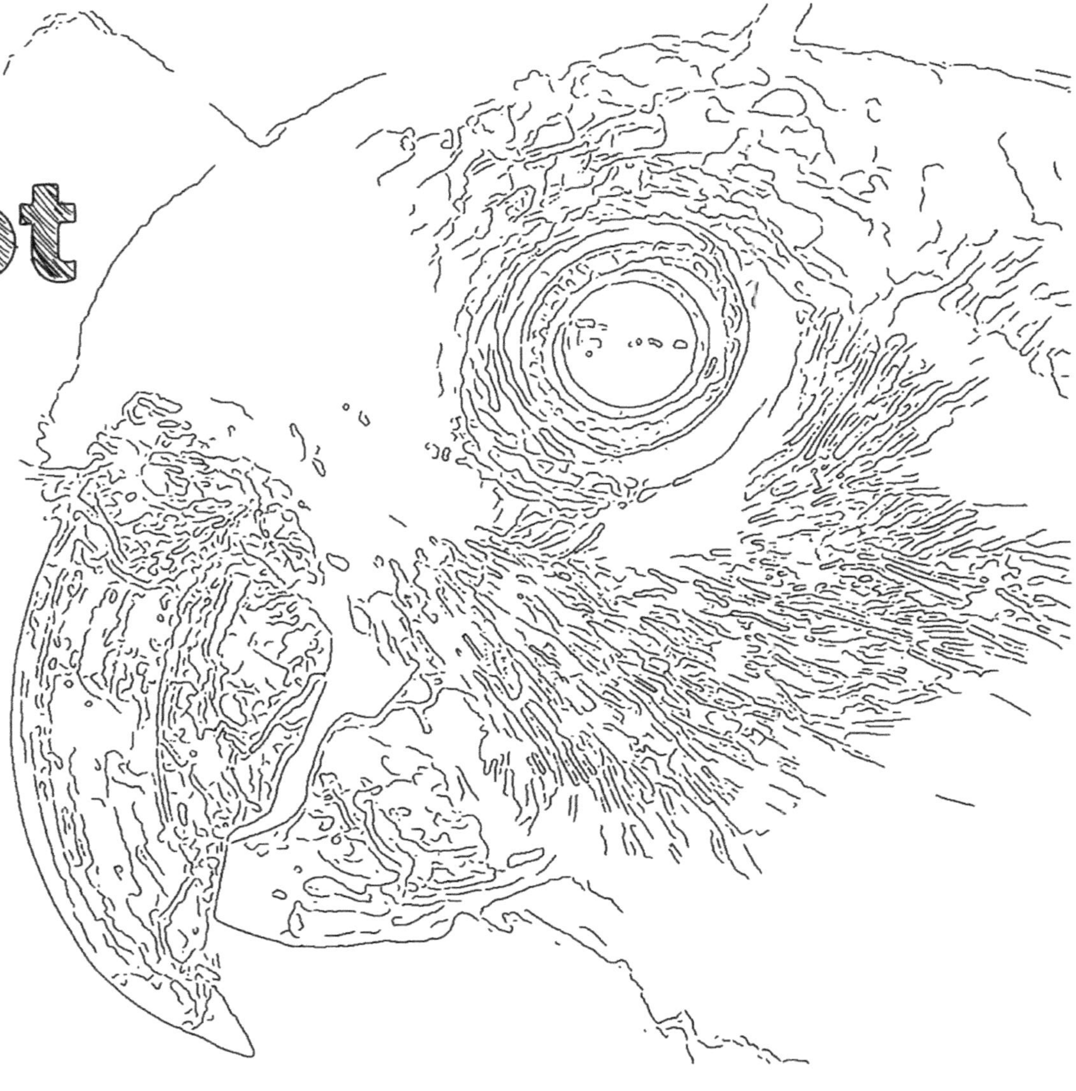

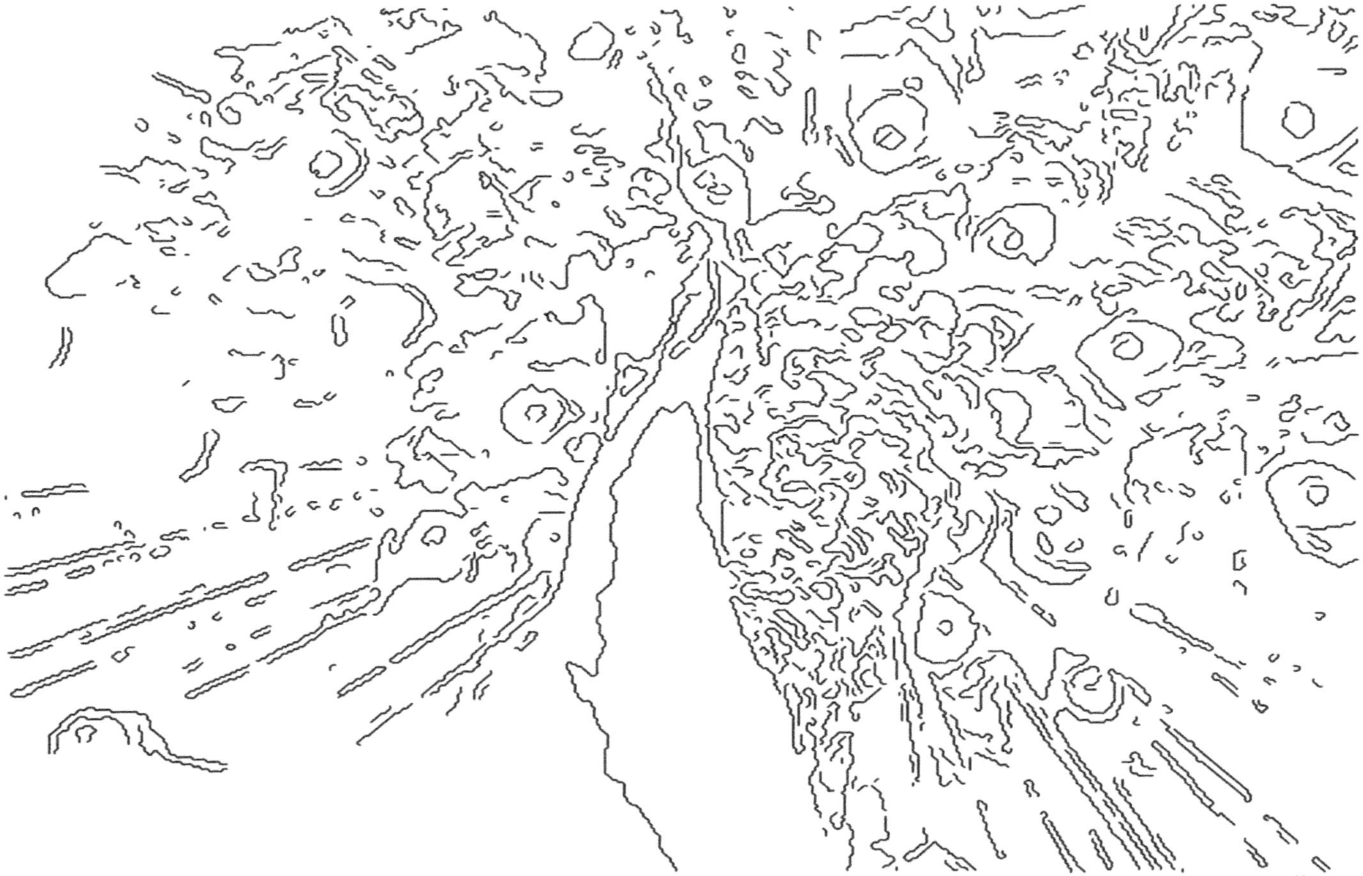

Peacock

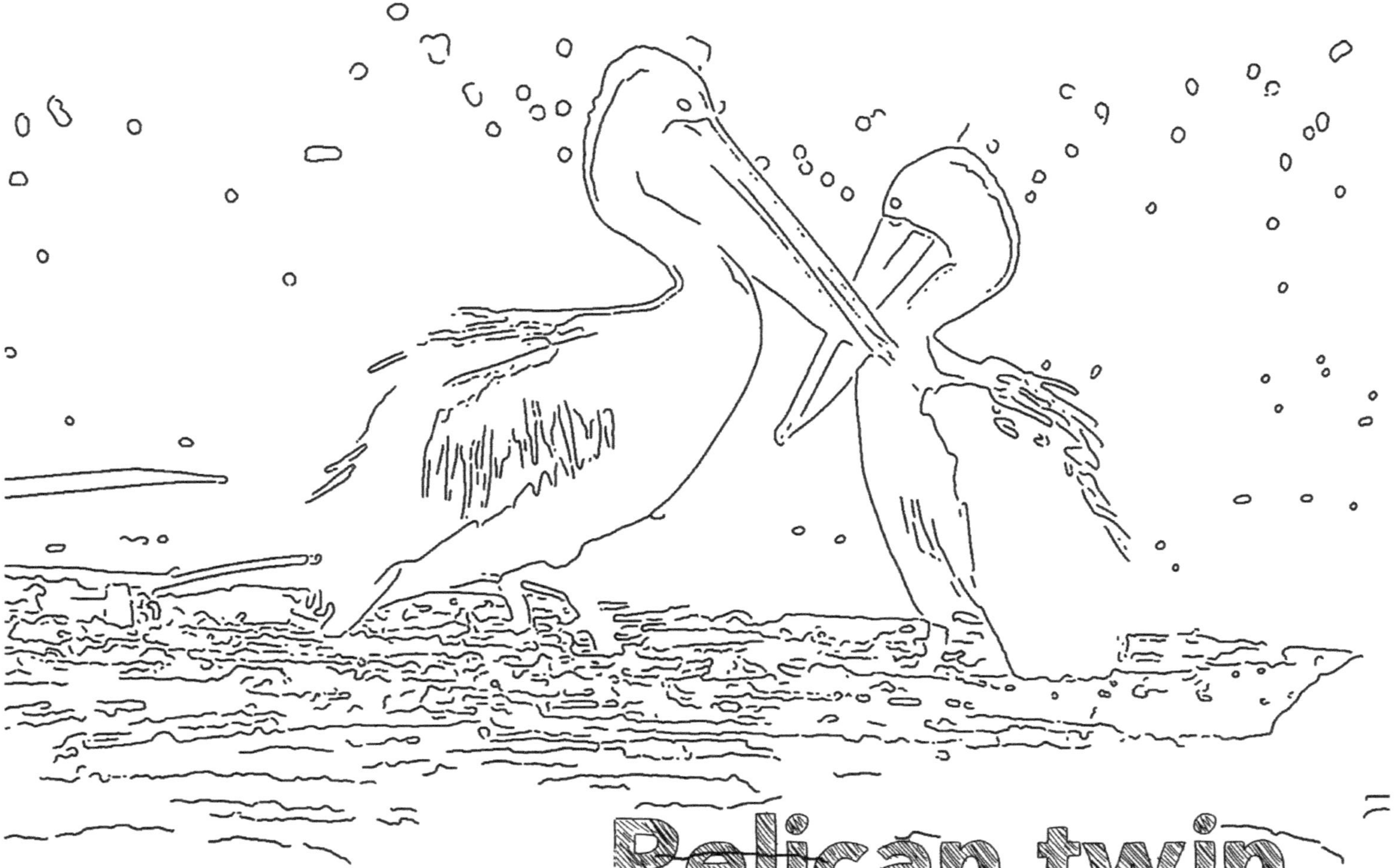

Pelican twin

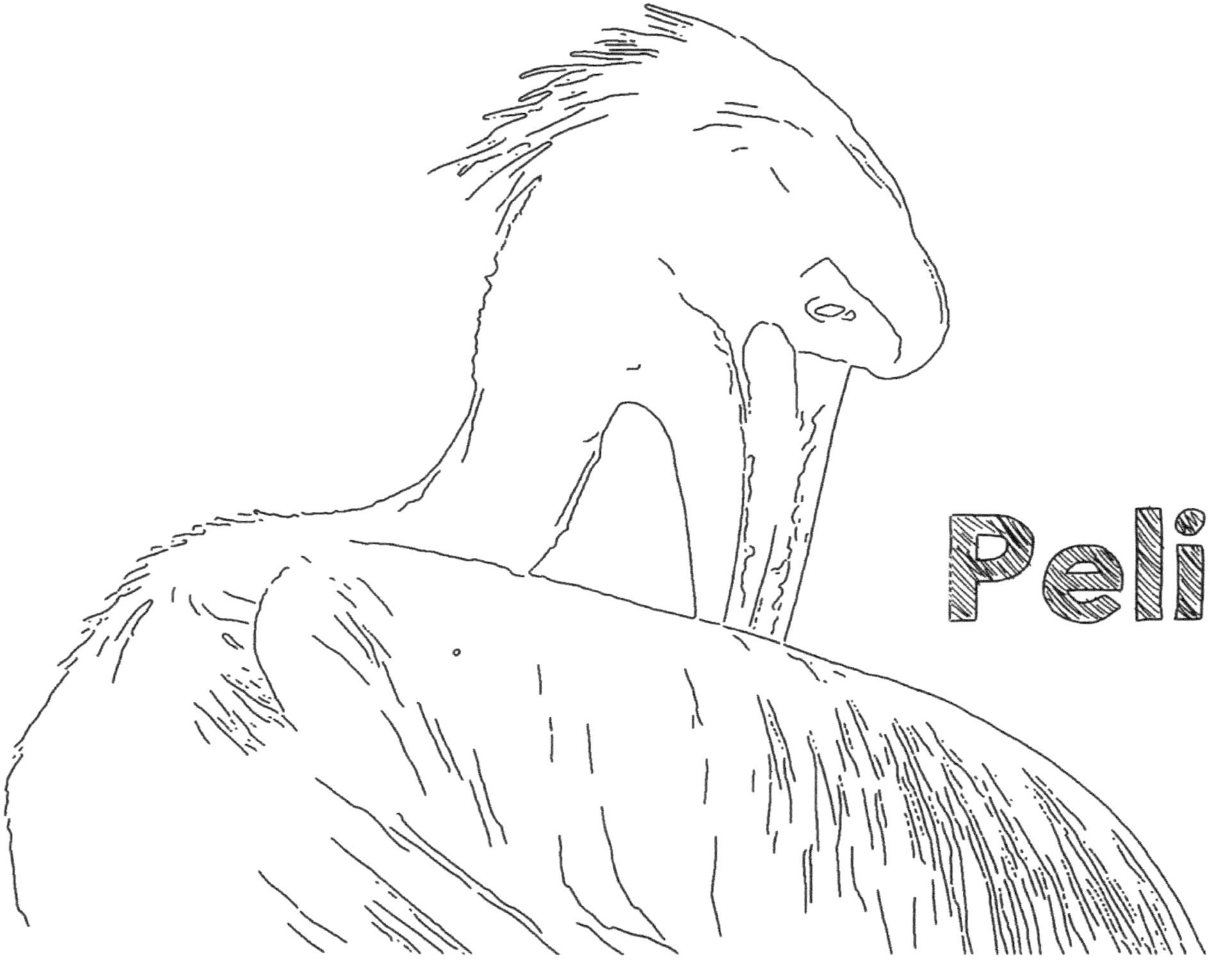

Pelican

Ravin

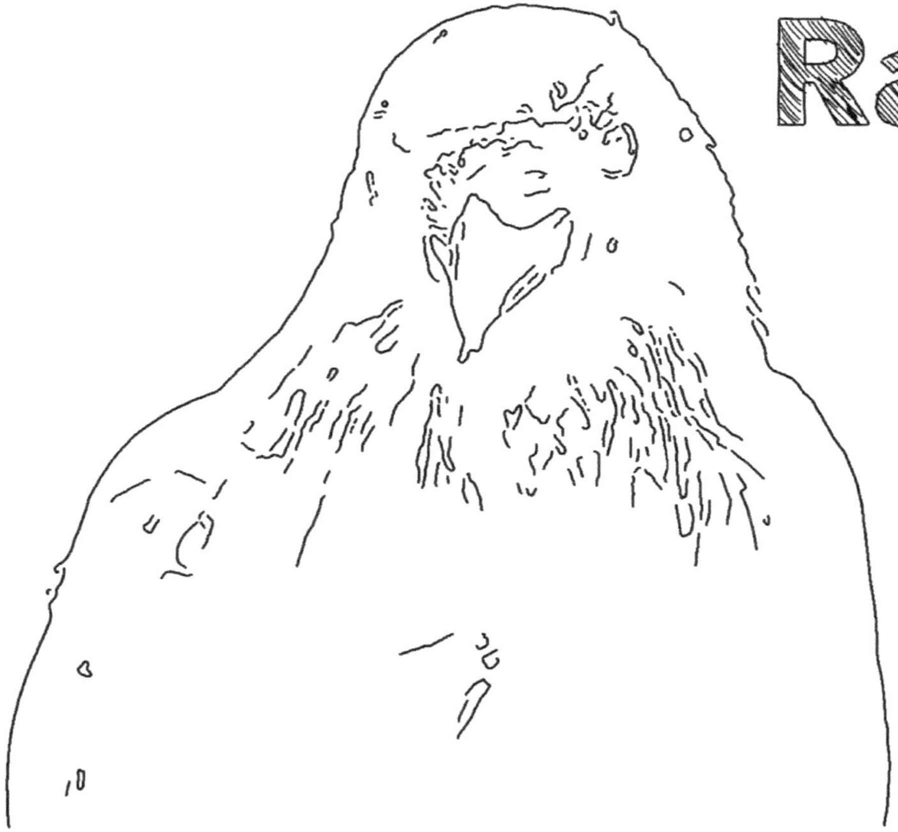

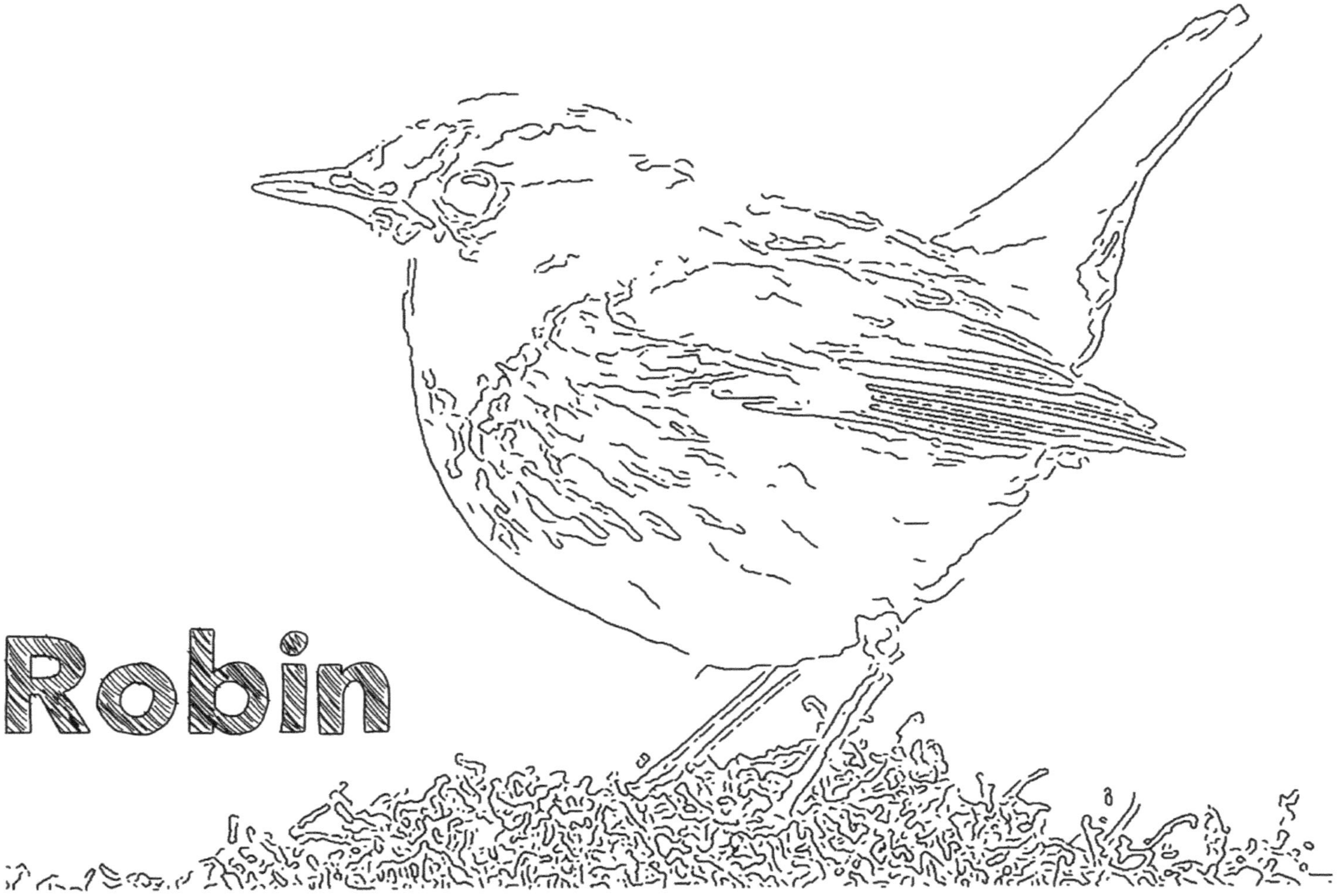

Robin

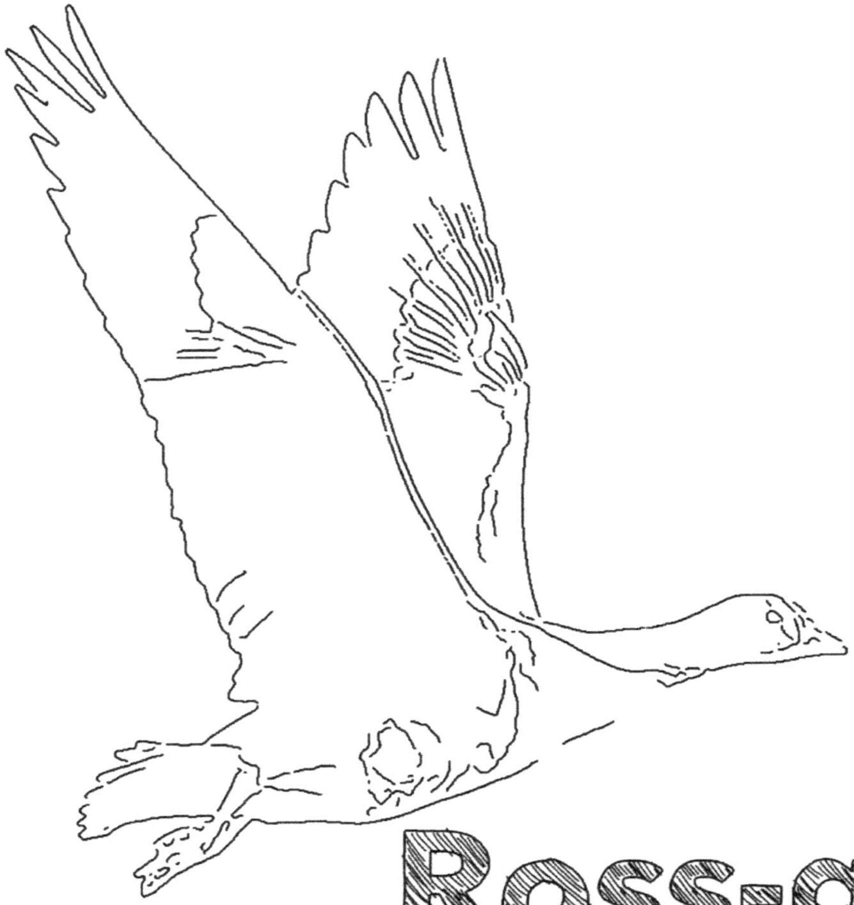

Ross-goose

Sacred-kingfisher

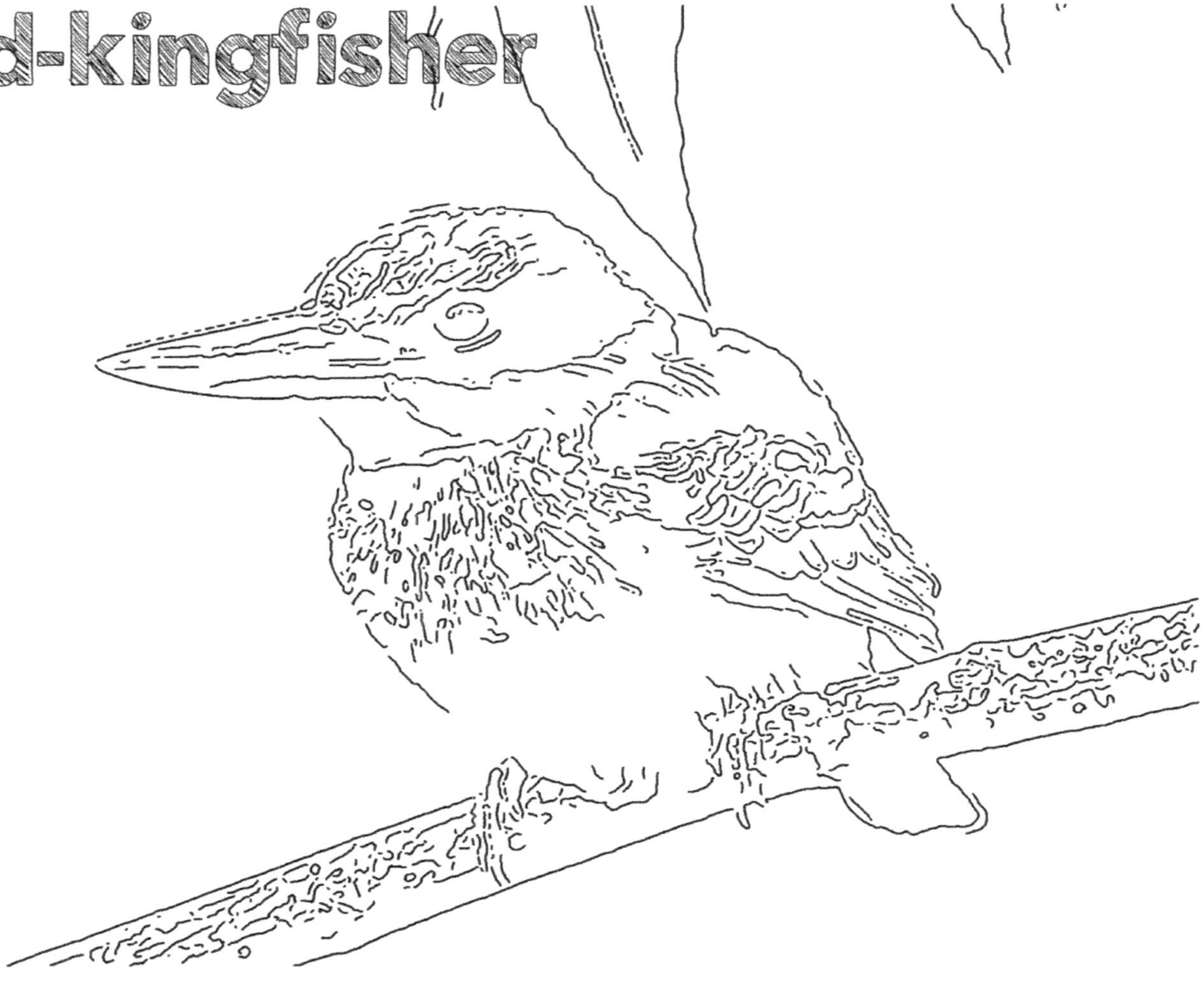

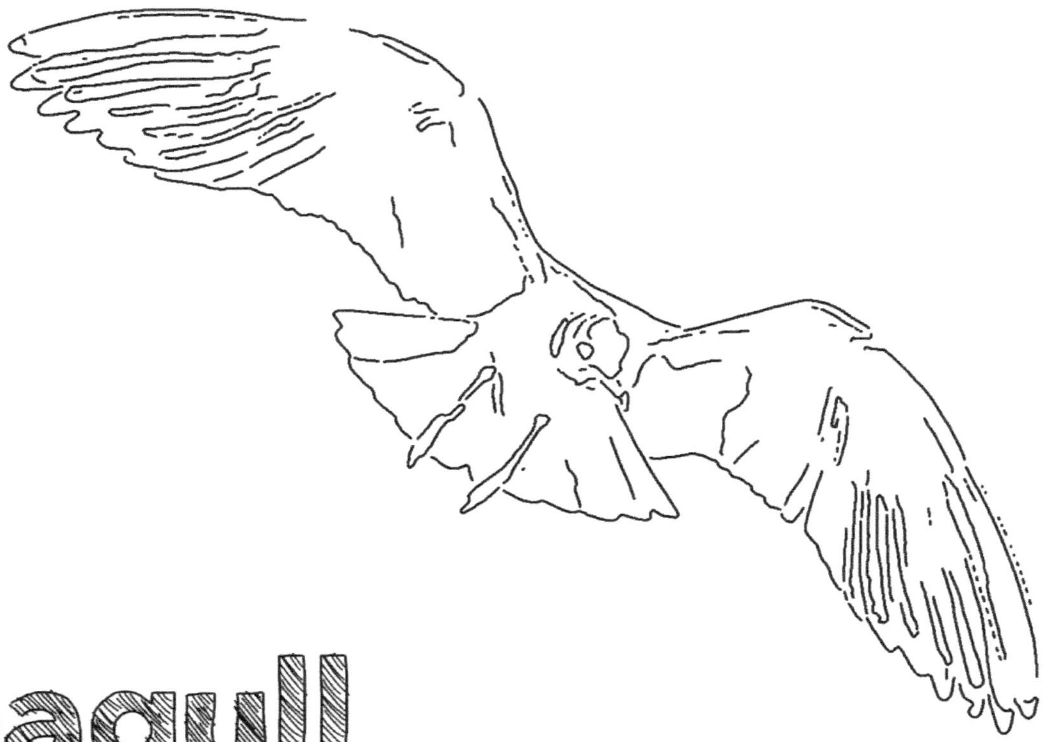

Seagull

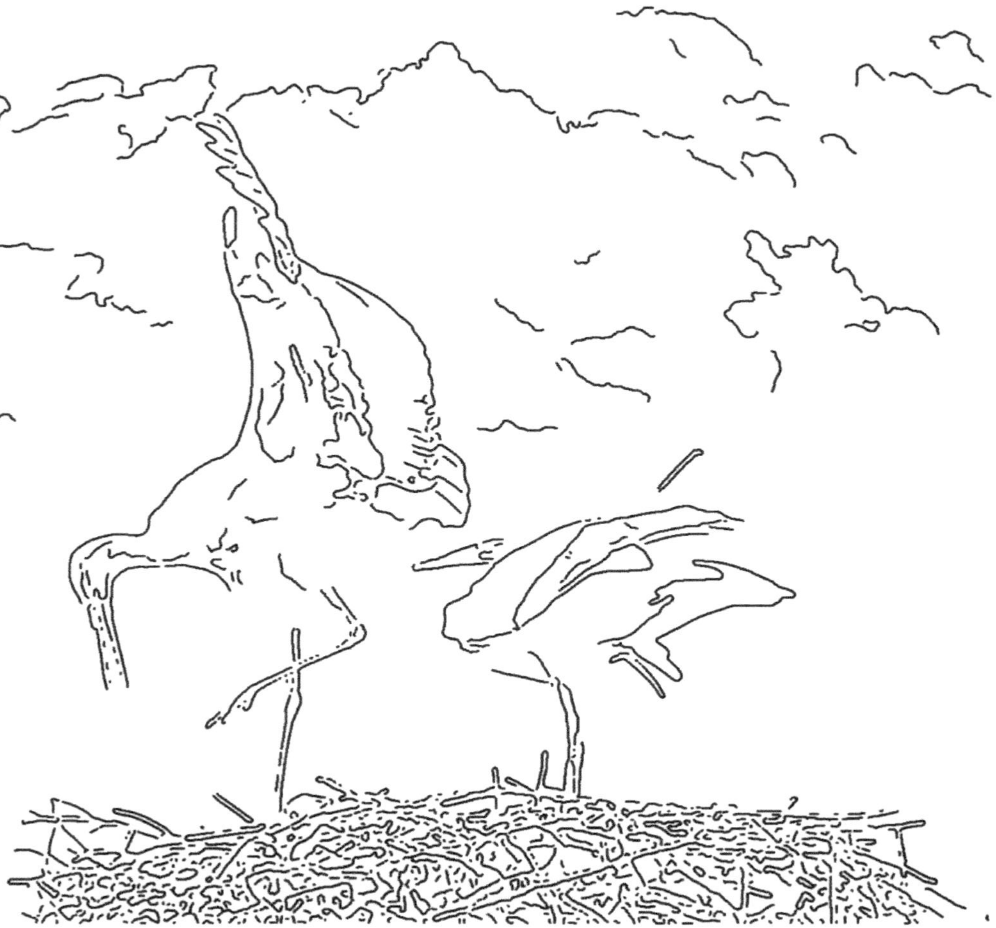

Stork

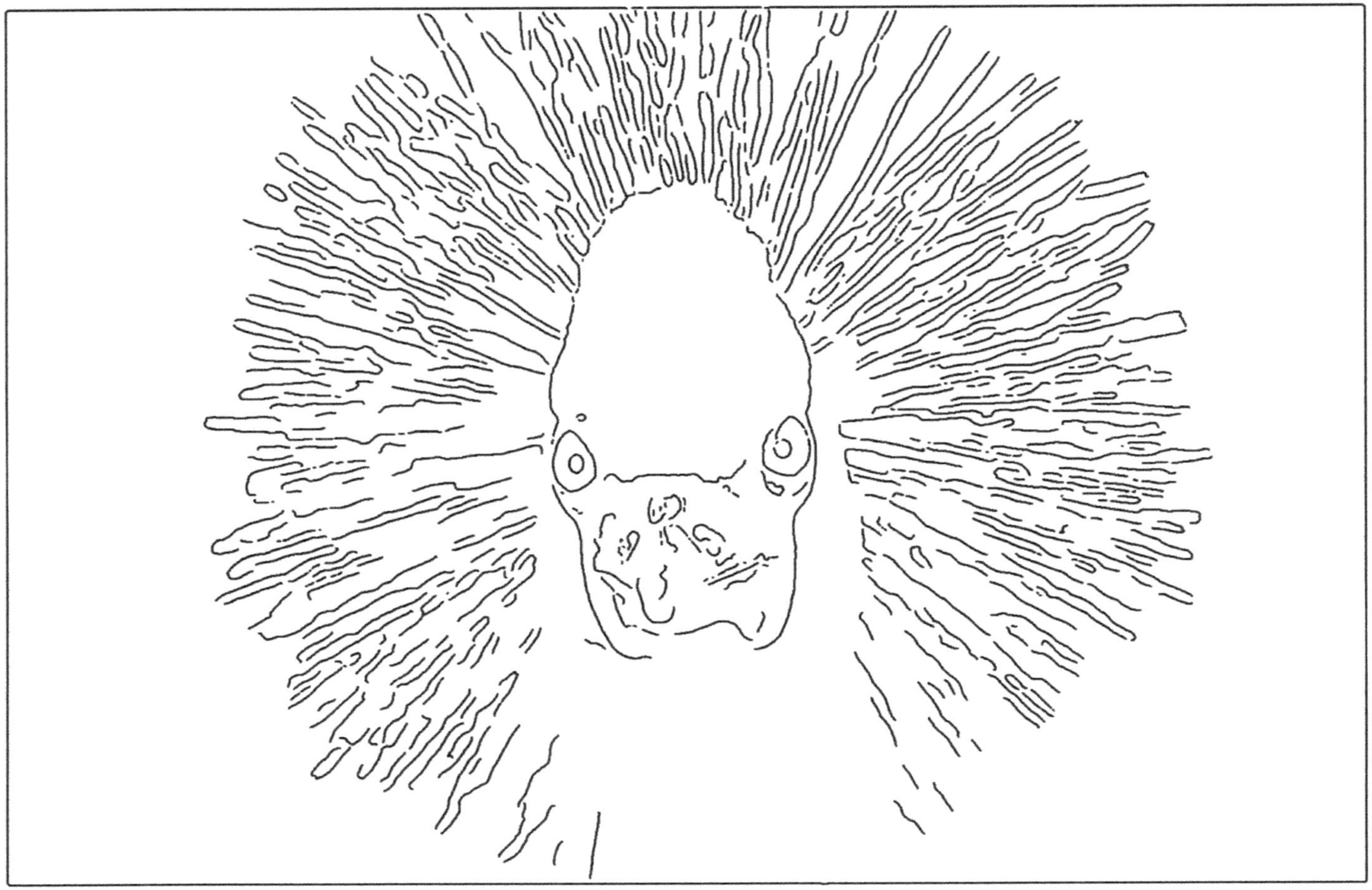

I don't know bird name..

Thank you

www.ingramcontent.com/pod-product-compliance
Lightning Source LLC
Chambersburg PA
CBHW080632190526
45169CB00009B/3368